THE MOSQUITO

Tundra Books, an imprint of Penguin Random House Canada Young Readers, a Penguin Random House Company

Library and Archives Canada Cataloguing in Publication

Title: The mosquito / Elise Gravel.
Other titles: Moustique. English
Names: Gravel, Elise, author.
Series: Gravel, Elise. Petits dégoûtants. English.
Description: Series statement: Disgusting critters | Translation of: Le moustique.
Identifiers: Canadiana (print) 20190141646 | Canadiana (ebook) 20190141697 | ISBN 9780735266452 (hardcover) | ISBN 9780735266469 (EPUB)
Subjects: LCSH: Mosquitoes—Juvenile literature.
Classification: LCC QL536 .G7213 2020 | DDC j595.77/2—dc23

Published simultaneously in the United States of America by Tundra Books of Northern New York, an imprint of Penguin Random House Canada Young Readers, a Penguin Random House Company

Library of Congress Control Number: 2019944407

English edition edited by Samantha Swenson
Designed by Elise Gravel and Tundra Books
The artwork in this book was rendered digitally.

Printed and bound in China

www.penguinrandomhouse.ca

1 2 3 4 5   24 23 22 21 20

Penguin Random House
TUNDRA BOOKS

Elise Gravel

THE MOSQUITO

HEY-O!

tundra

Ladies and gentlemen, let me introduce

THE MOSQUITO.

Around here, we call her

SKEETER.

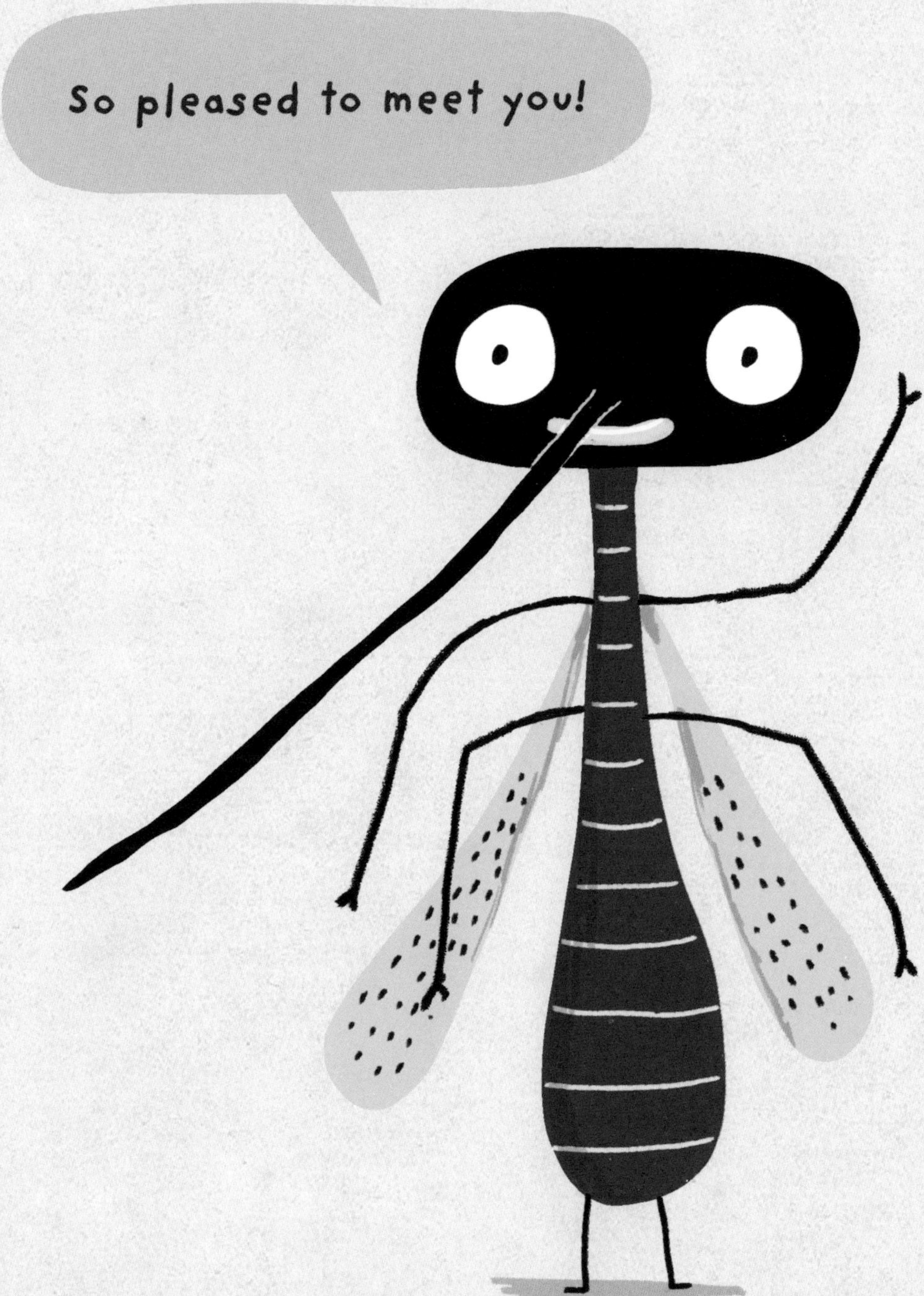
So pleased to meet you!

The mosquito is an insect from the Diptera order, just like the fly. There are more than 3,000 mosquito species! We can find her everywhere on the planet, and everywhere on the planet, she bugs us.

That's because she

STINGS!

Jdi pryč!

Vai-te embora!

Geh weg

Kuro patapata

Vattene

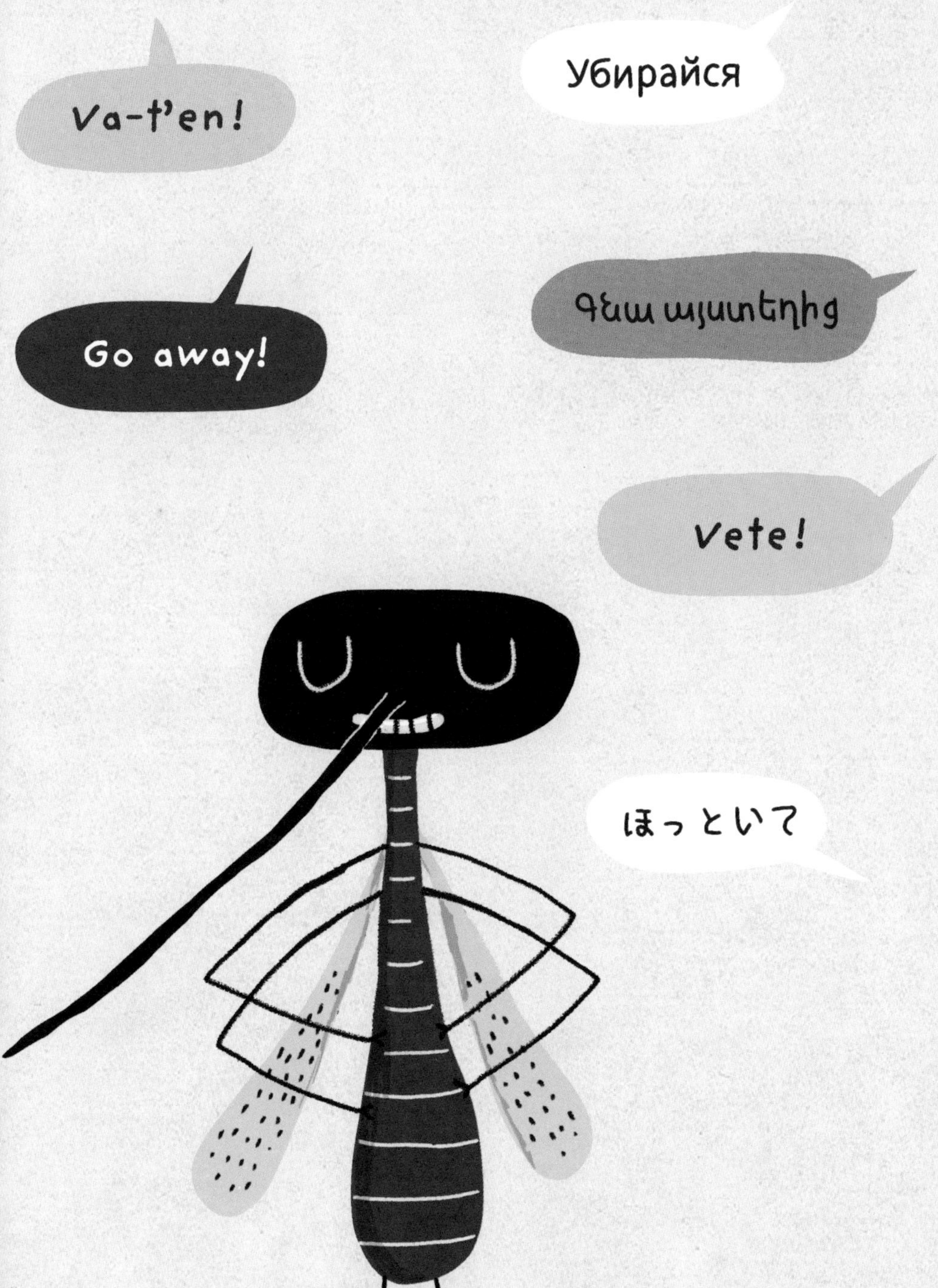
Va-t'en!
Убирайся
Go away!
Գնա այստեղից
Vete!
ほっといて

Only the female mosquito stings.
She needs the protein in animal
blood to produce

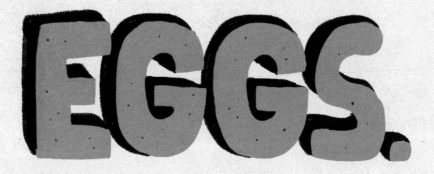

Male mosquitoes eat flower nectar
and other forms of sugar.

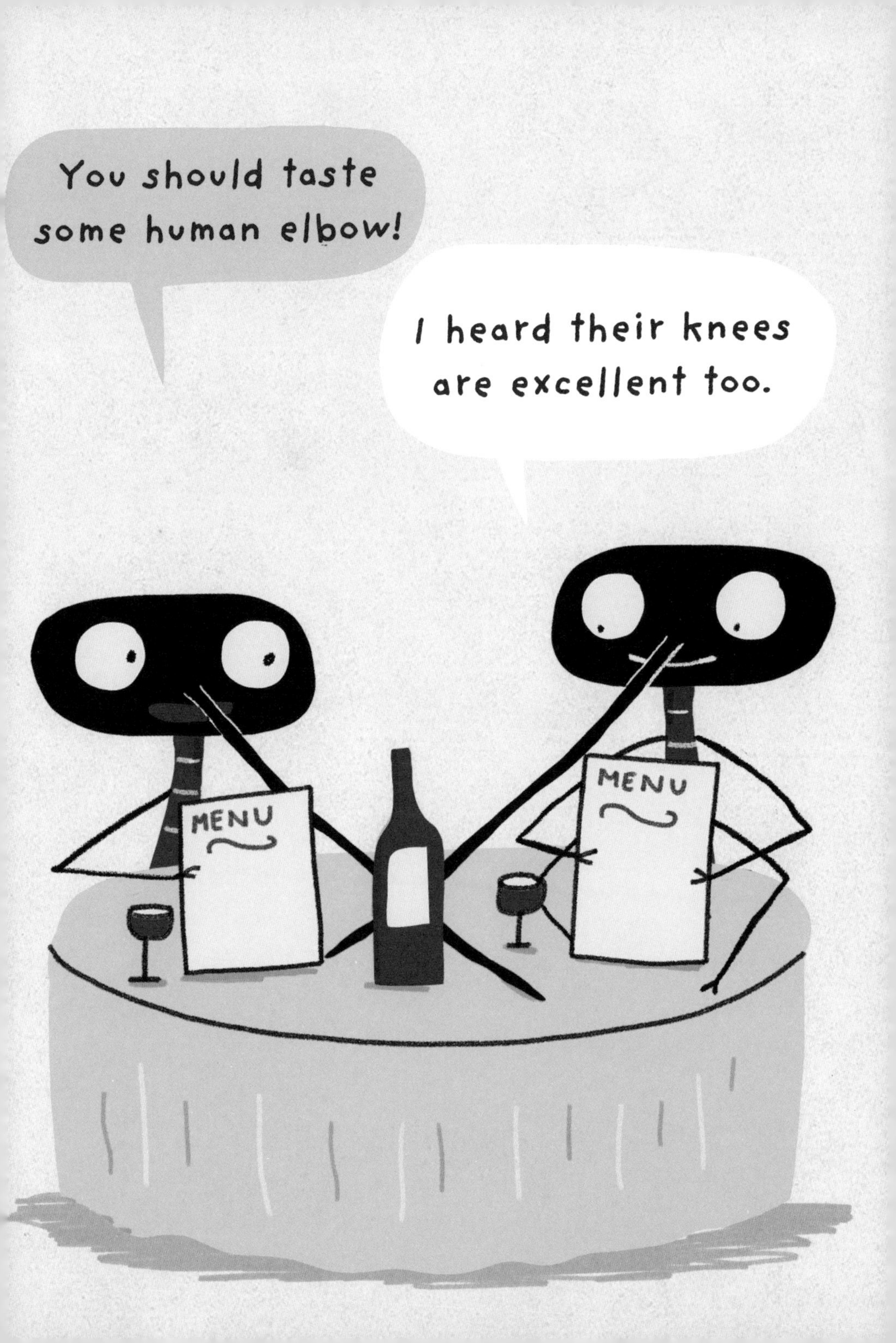
You should taste some human elbow!
I heard their knees are excellent too.
MENU
MENU

The mosquito bites us with a long trunk called a

PROBOSCIS.

She finds a blood vessel with it and sucks our blood!

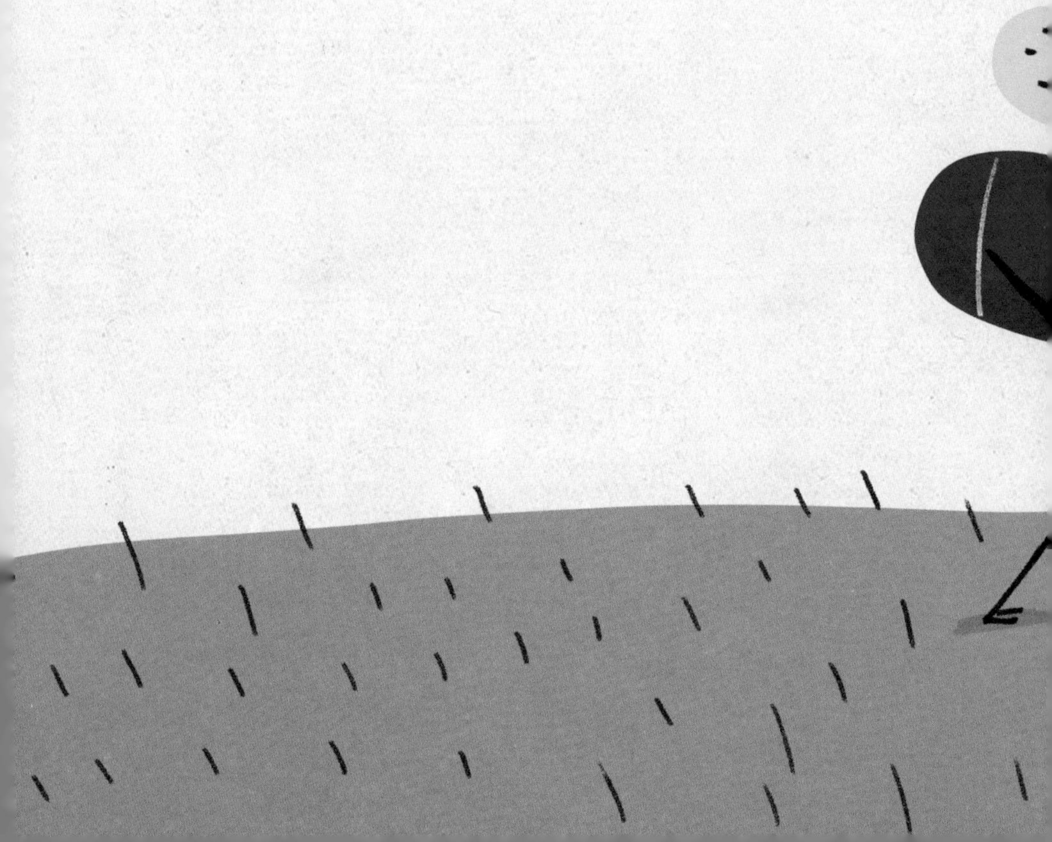

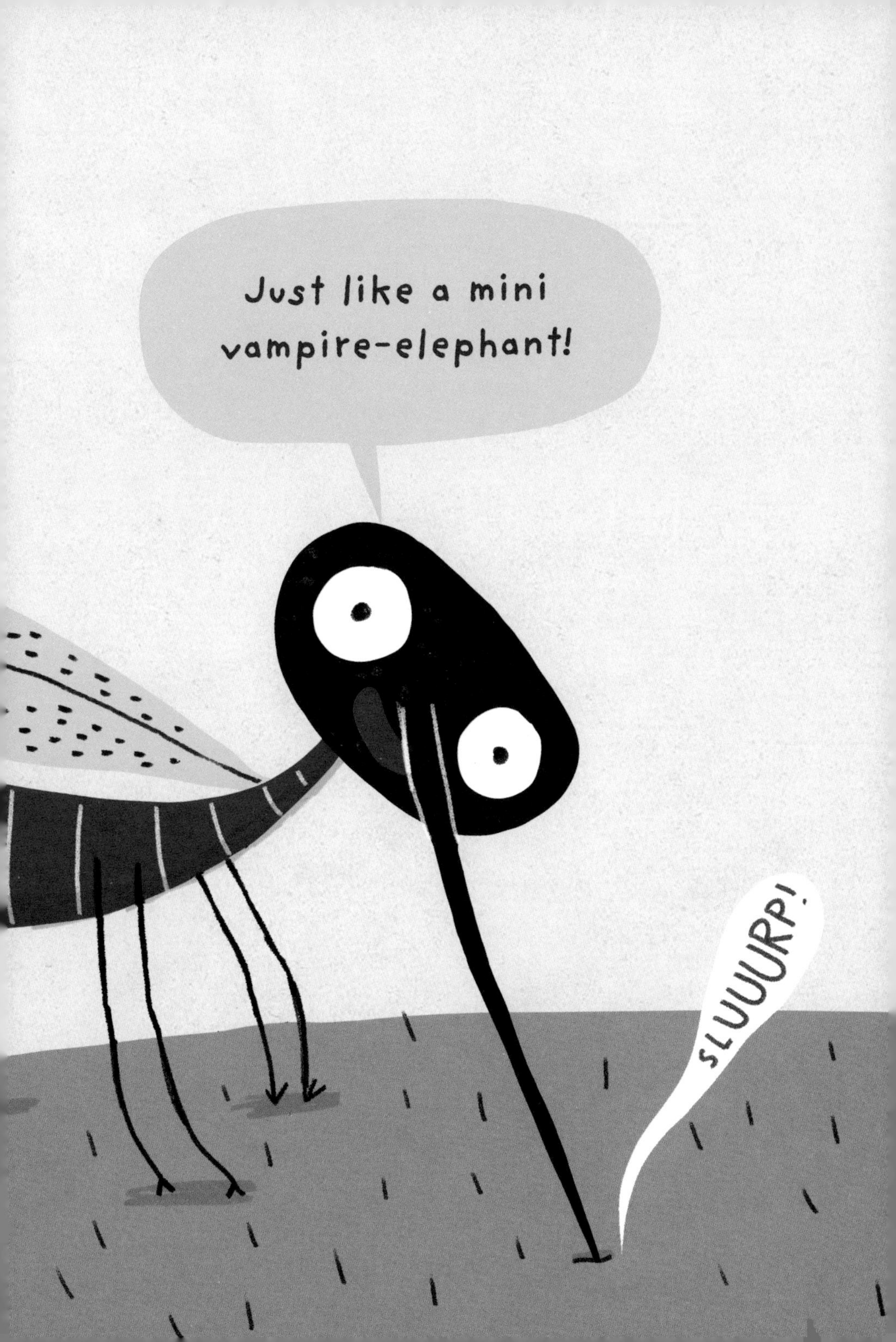
Just like a mini vampire-elephant!
SLUUURP!

She can find us by detecting the

CARBON DiOXiDE

that we emit when we breathe. She can also smell us and feel the heat from our bodies.

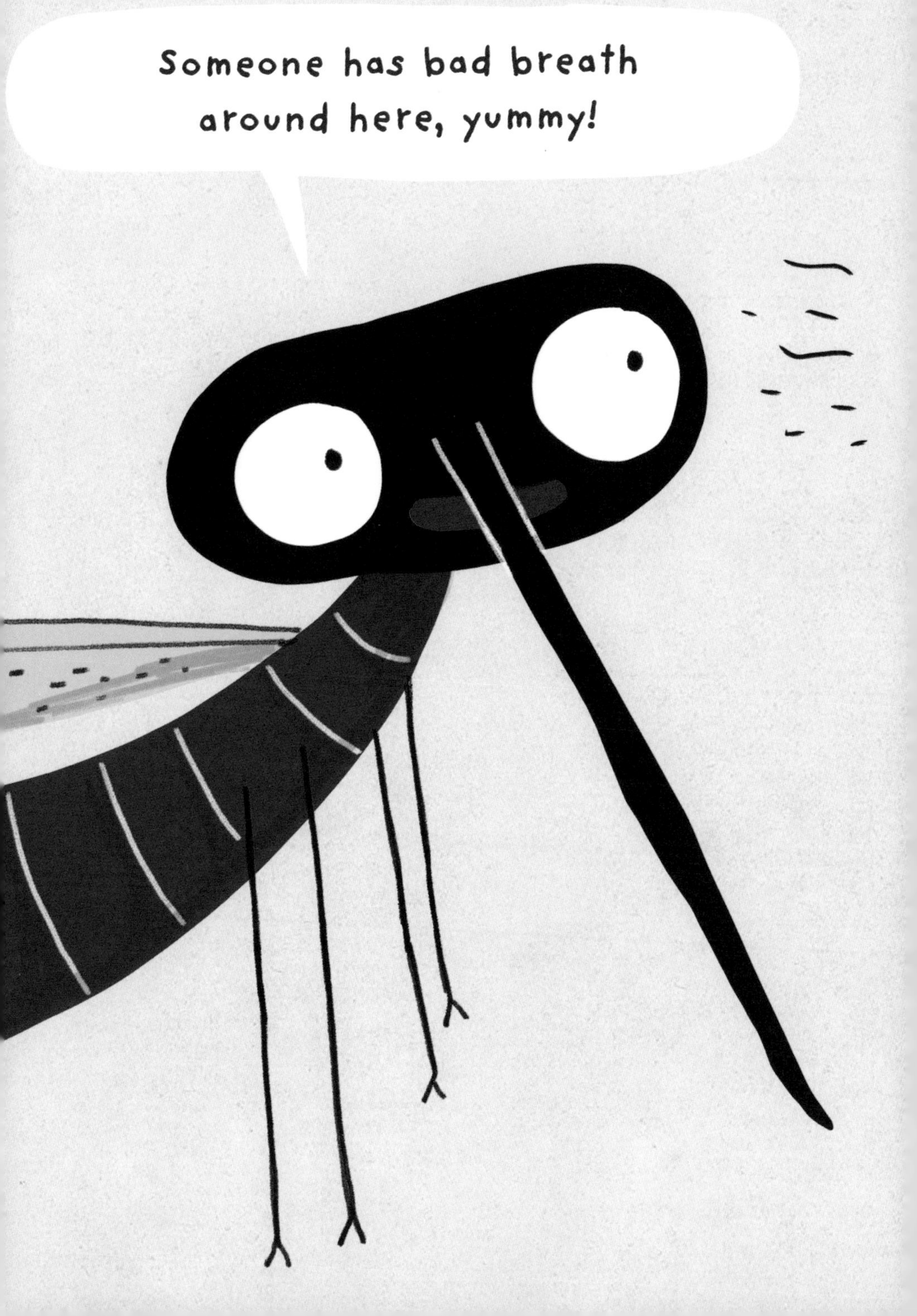
Someone has bad breath around here, yummy!

When she stings, the mosquito injects a bit of

SALIVA

in our skin. This saliva prevents us from feeling the sting so she can sneakily drink our blood and fly away before we notice!

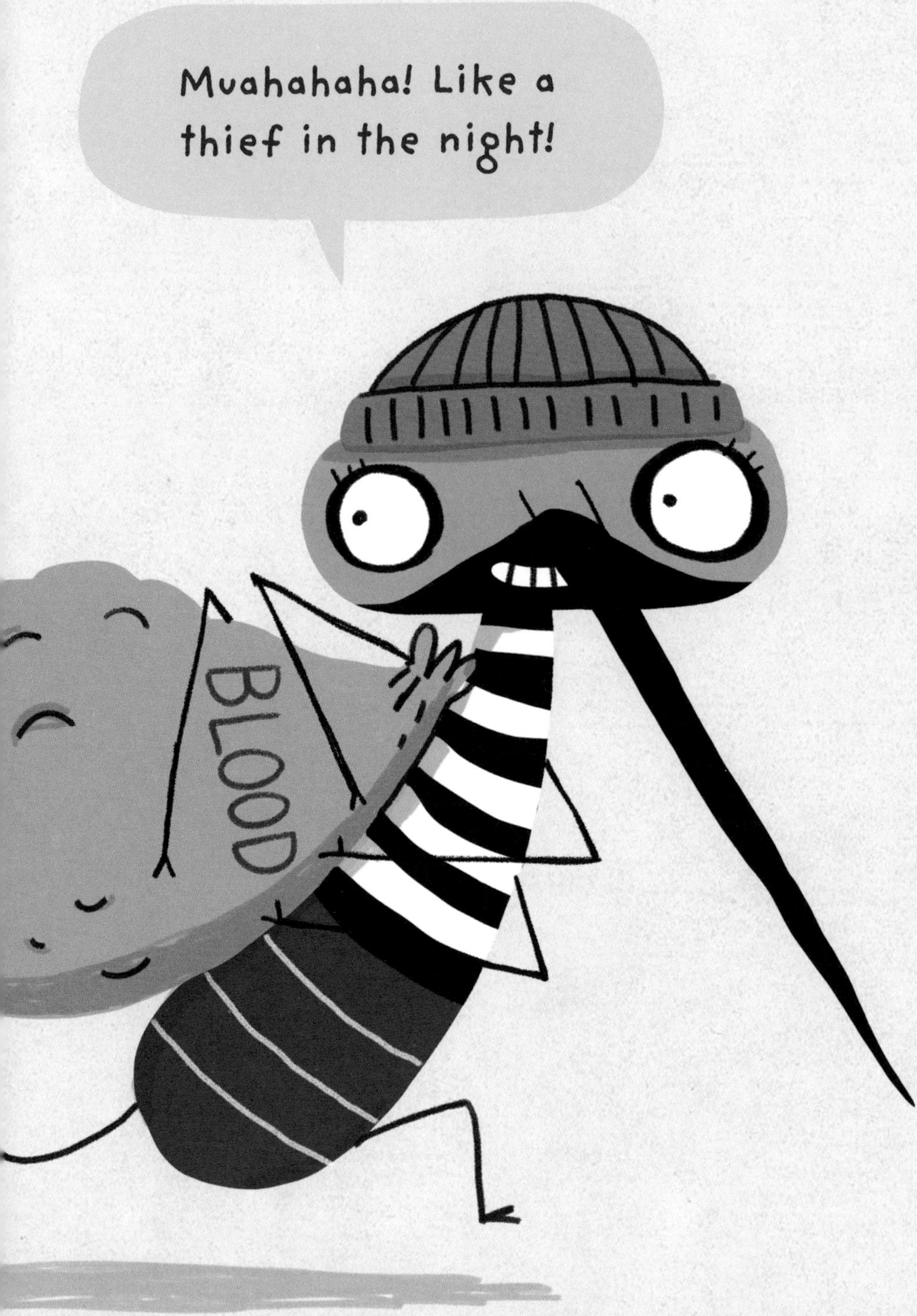
Muahahaha! Like a thief in the night!
BLOOD

A few minutes after, a little

BUMP

appears: it's our skin reacting to the saliva. This itchy spot will disappear within a few days.

Not bad, eh? I'm practicing my signature.

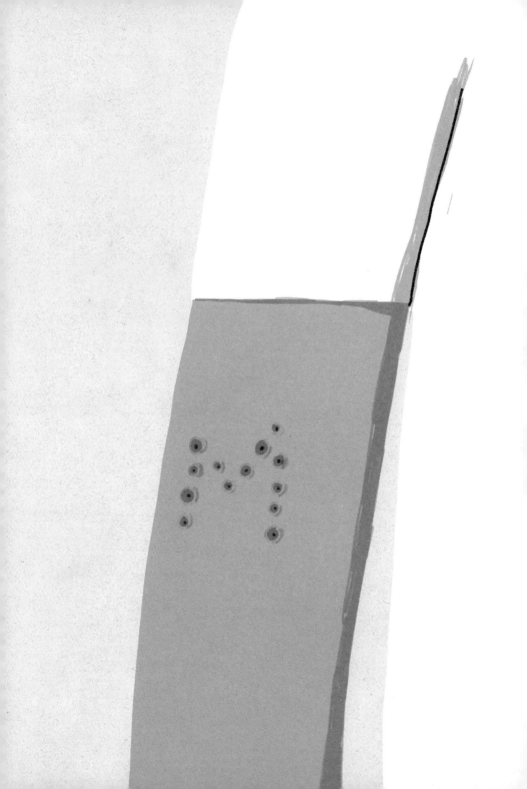

The mosquito makes a very annoying

BUZZING

sound thanks to her wings that flap up to 800 times per second.

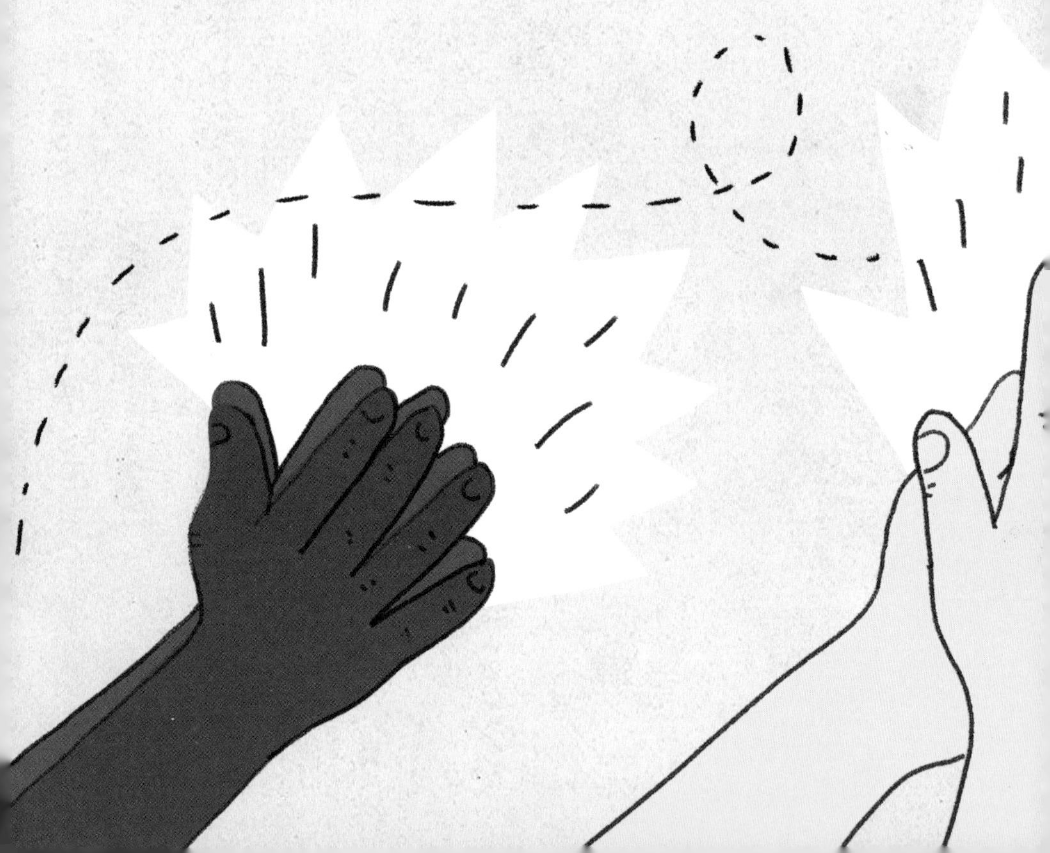

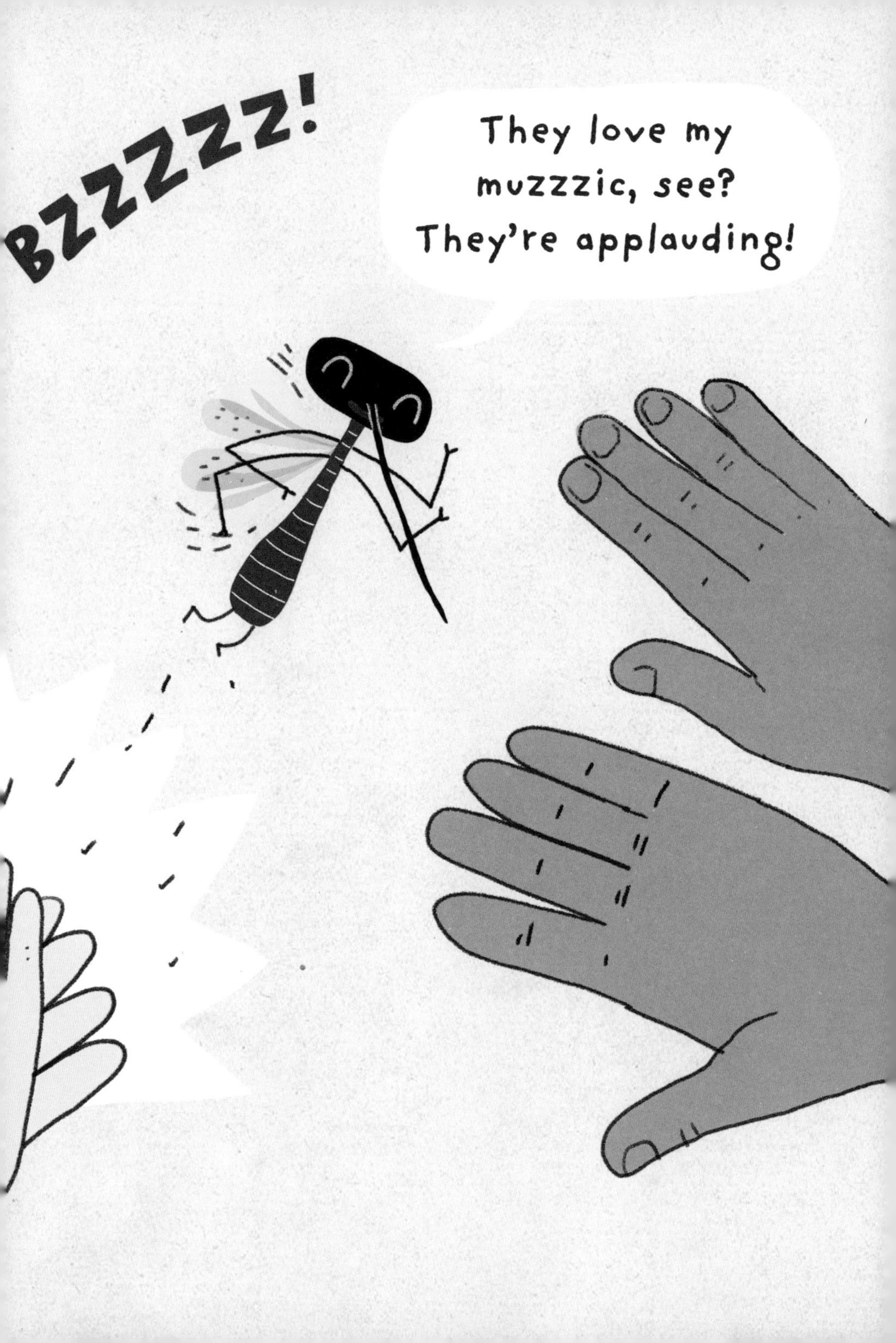
BZZZZZ!
They love my muzzzic, see? They're applauding!

Despite these super-fast wings, the mosquito flies very slowly. If all flying insects had a race, the mosquito would come

DEAD LAST.

At least I participated!

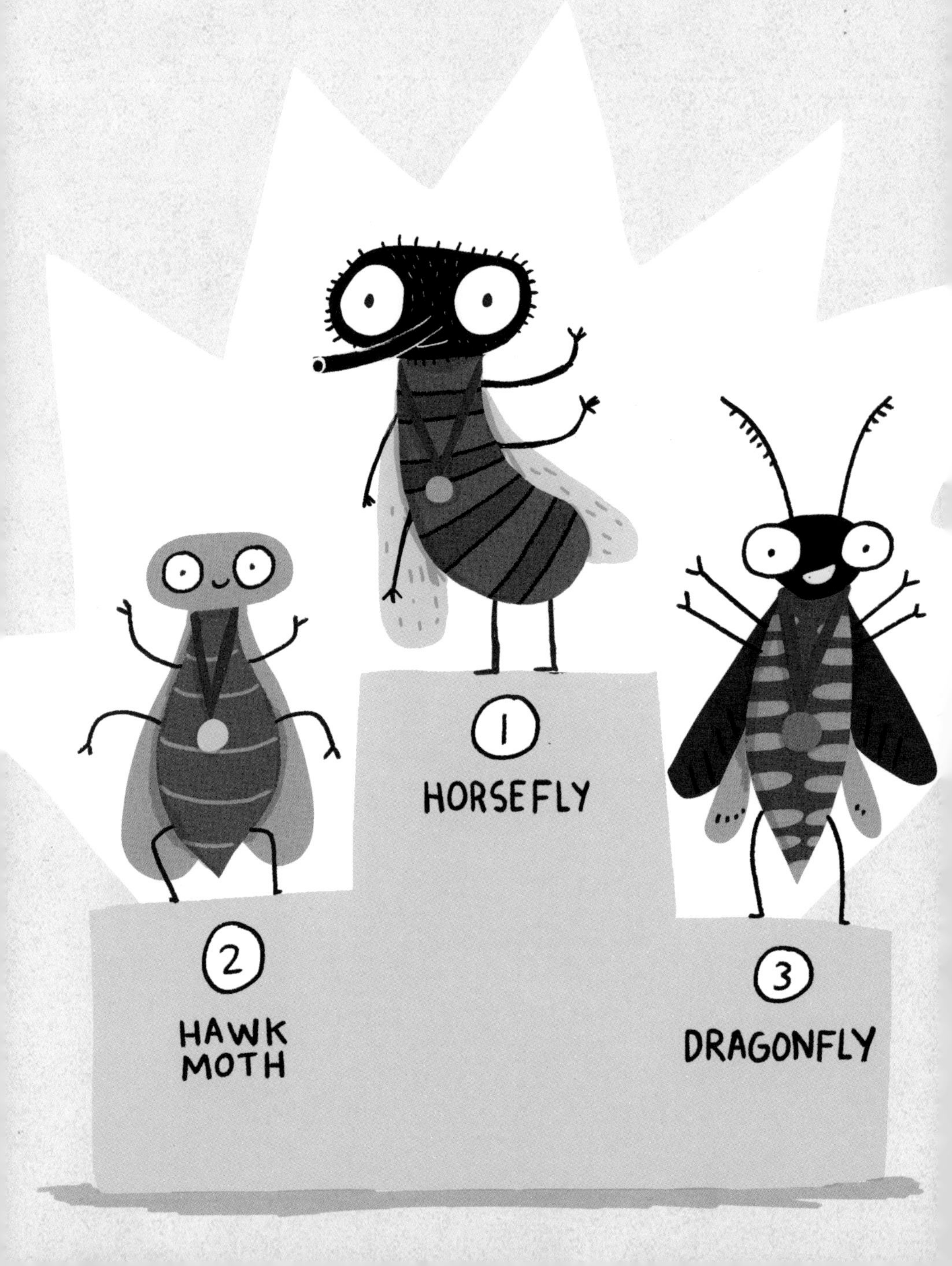
1
HORSEFLY
2
HAWK
MOTH
3
DRAGONFLY

In warm countries, the mosquito can infect people with dangerous diseases such as malaria. She might be tiny, but the mosquito is more

DANGEROUS

to humans than sharks or lions!

Jealouzzz??

The female mosquito lays her eggs in stagnant water: a marsh, a pond, a bucket of rainwater, even a puddle is enough water for her to make babies. She can lay up to

400

eggs at a time!

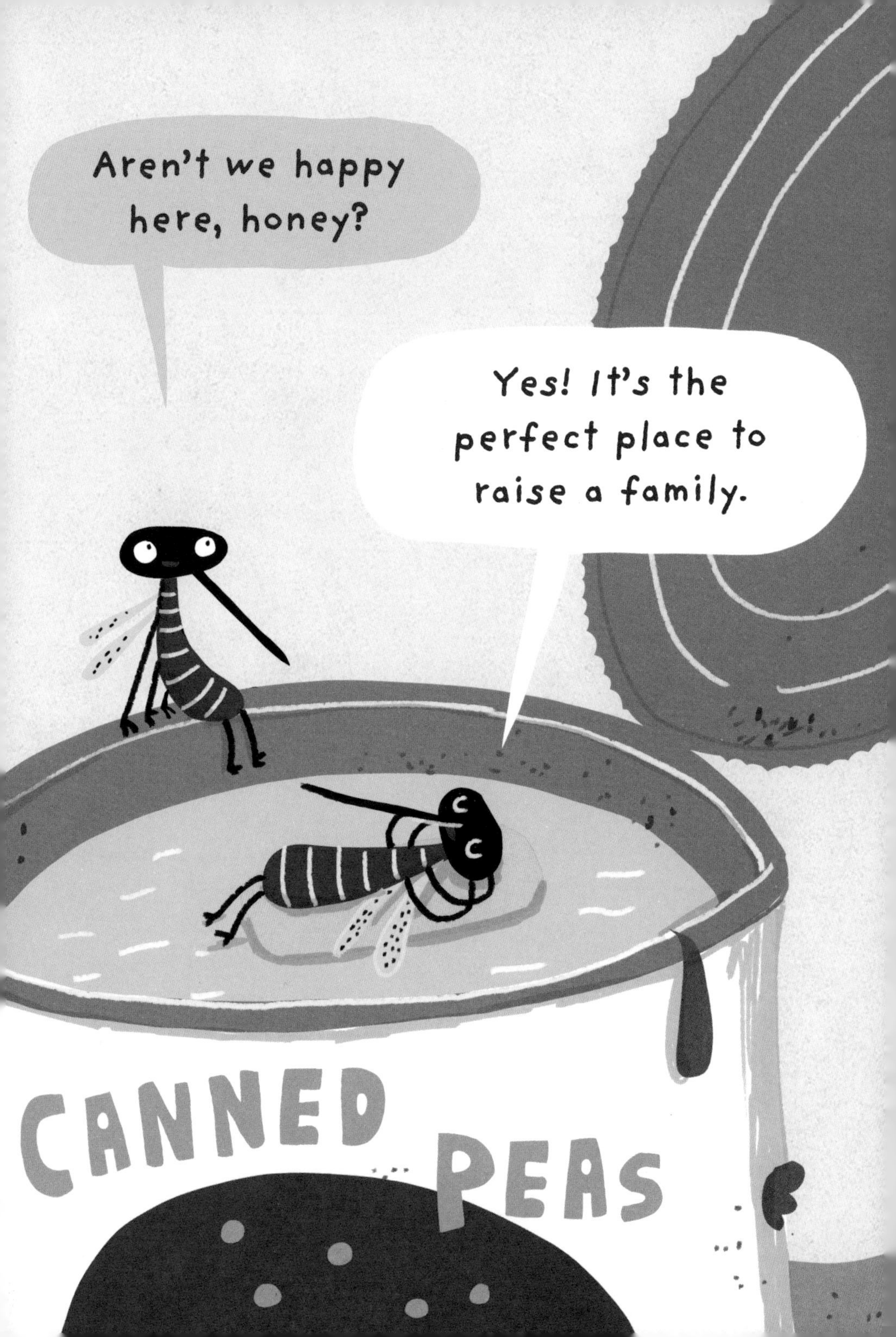
Aren't we happy here, honey?
Yes! It's the perfect place to raise a family.
CANNED PEAS

The mosquito egg hatches in the water and the

LARVA

comes out, looking for a snack. After spending some time floating and eating, the larva becomes a pupa. The pupa stays in the water, but still needs to breathe air, so it stays on the surface of the water. Finally, a few weeks after hatching, the mosquito is an adult and is ready to sting you and lay eggs. Cute, right?

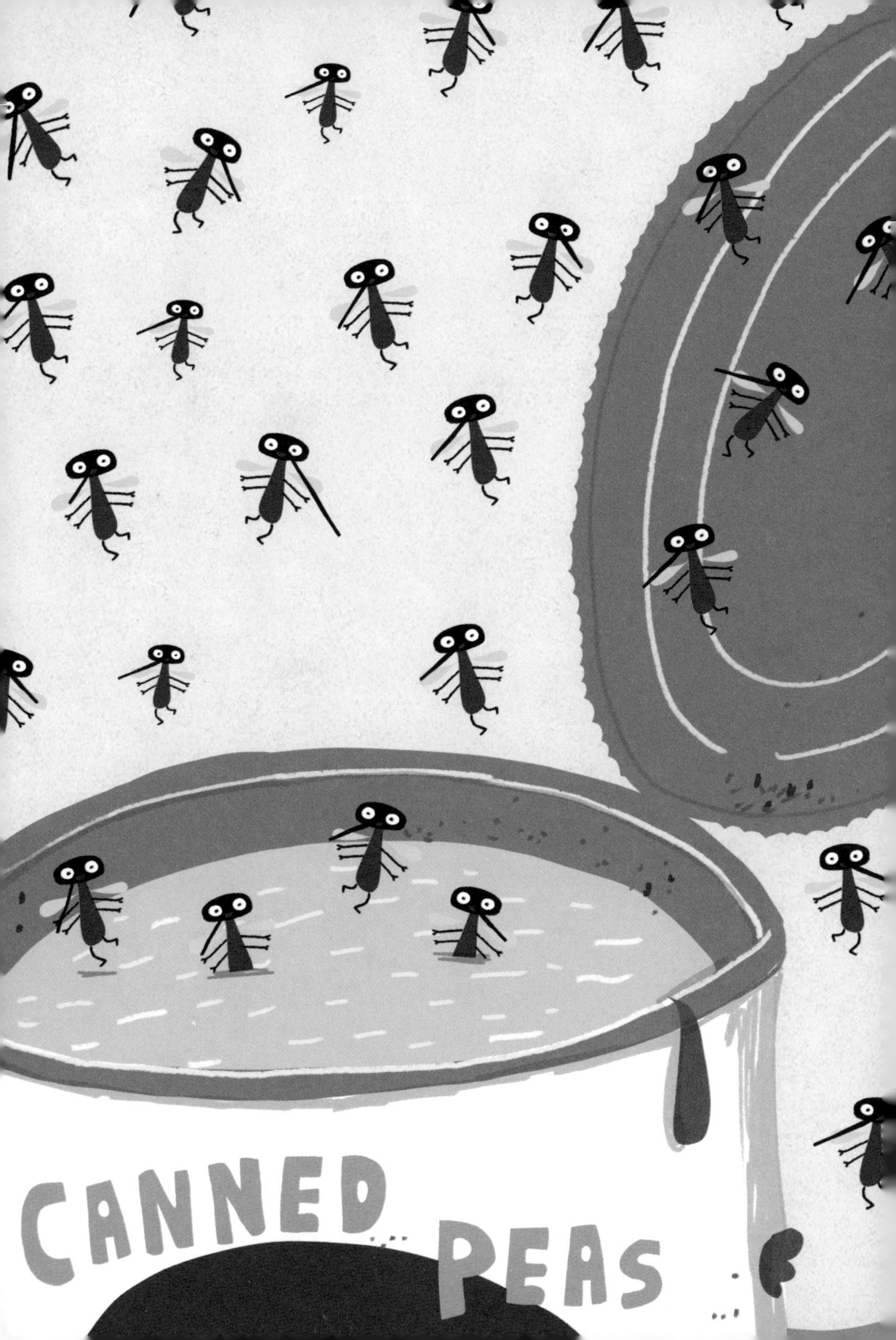
CANNED PEAS

The female mosquito can live between a few days and a few months if she's not eaten by a

PREDATOR

like the spider, the toad, the fish or the bat. Male mosquitoes only tend to live about 10 days. Sorry, guys! Since the female mosquito can hibernate, she will always be ready to greet us in the spring.

Hey there, long time no see! I missed you so much. Let me give you a little kiss!

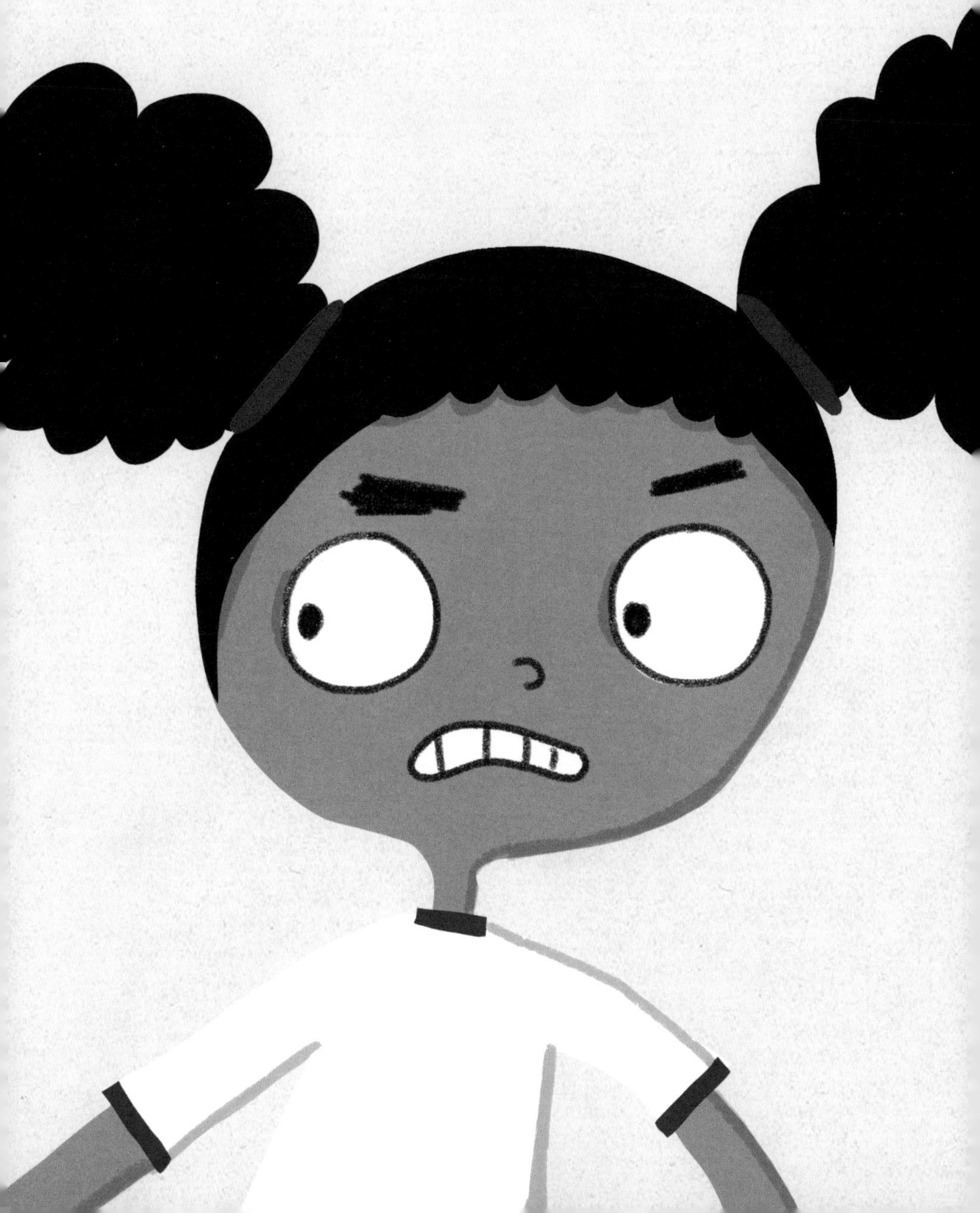

So if you don't want the mosquito's company that much, use bug repellent, wear

LONG SLEEVES

and long pants and make friends with a mosquito predator.

What, you don't like my new hat?

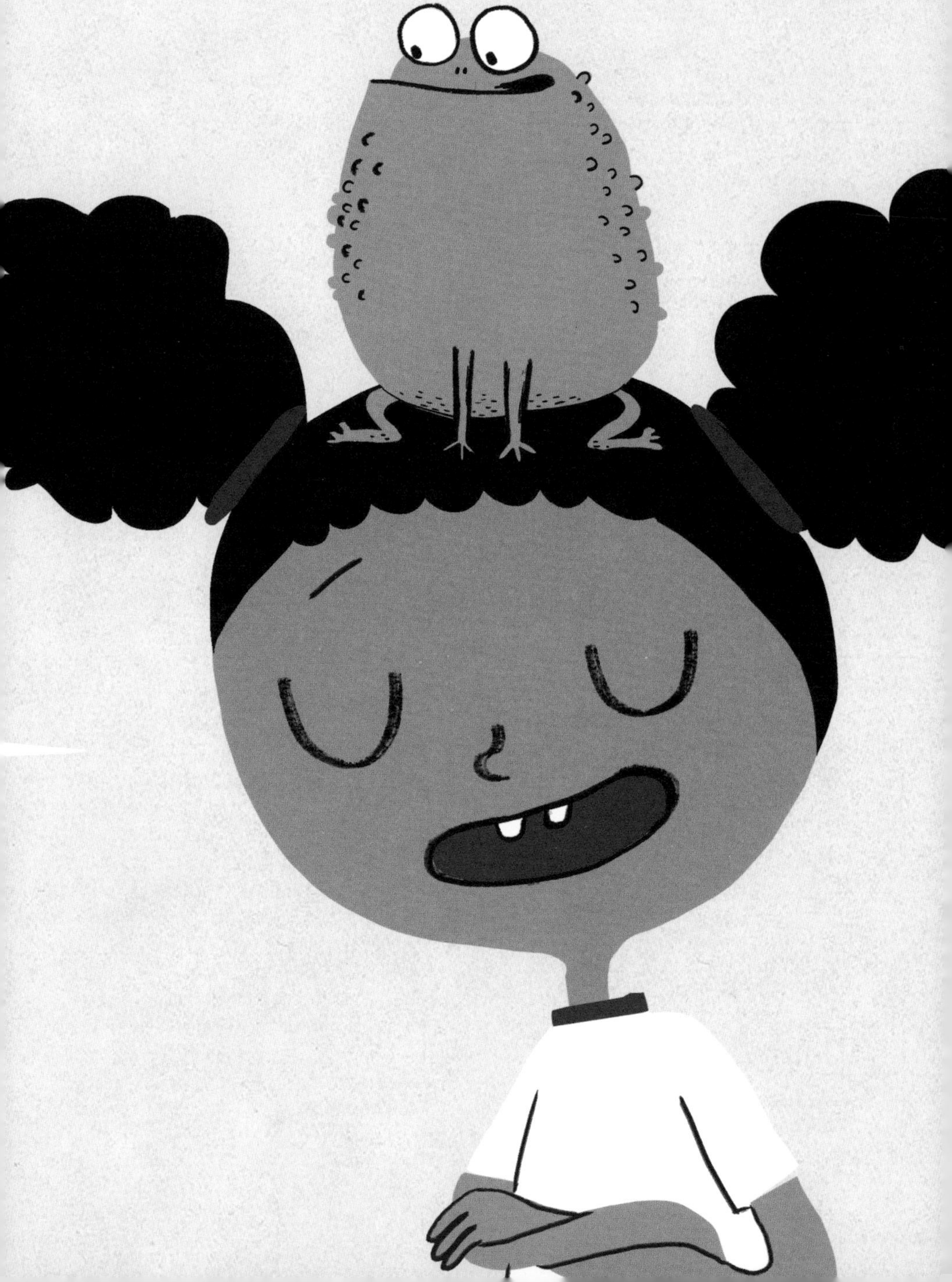

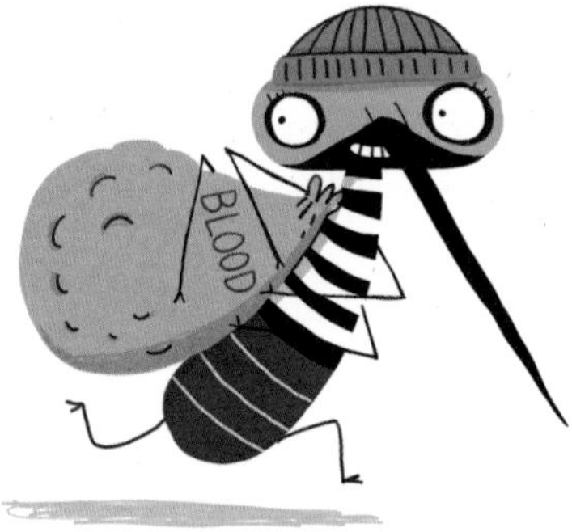
BLOOD

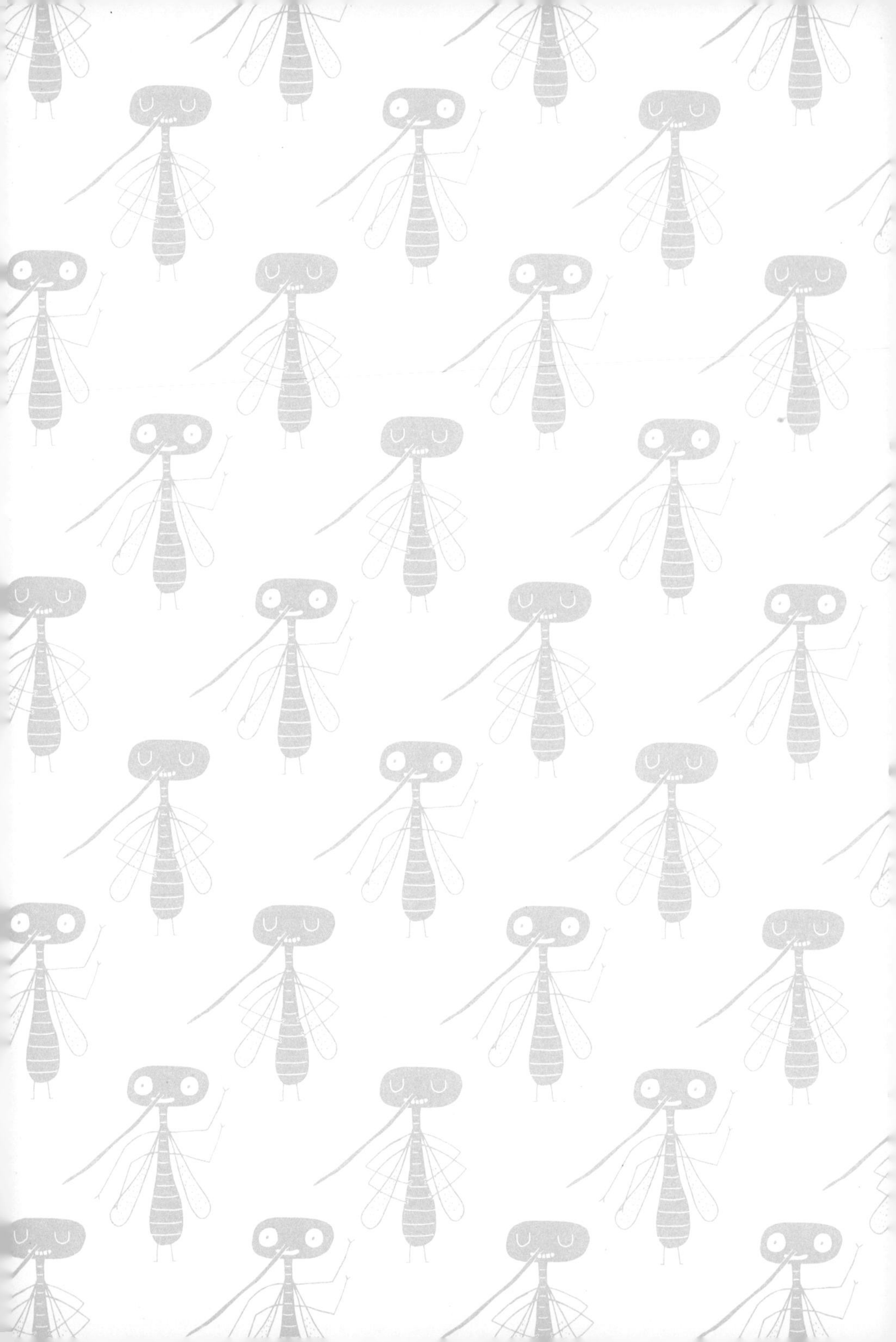